100 Original Artist Quotes

J. Bonegard

Vol. 1

J. BONEGARD

Copyright © 2024 J. Bonegard
All rights reserved. Published by Wundia Books.
Wundia and associated logos are trademarks and/or
registered trademarks.
Learn about the author @j.bonegard on
Facebook/Twitter/Instagram/Pinterest/Google+, and on the
web site www.jbonegard.com

Cover design – Oladunni Oladipo

No part of this publication may be published in whole or in
part, or stored in a retrieval system, or transmitted in any
form or by any means, electronic, mechanical, photocopying,
recording, or otherwise, without written permission of the
publisher. For information regarding permission, write to
Wundia Books, PO Box 446, Canton, MA 02021 USA.

First Printing, March 2024

____

PROLOGUE

As a writer who became an artist much later in life, I was drawn to the idea of including my musings as I share my artwork with the public. So far, I have been able to combine these two passions, using my paintings, installations, and other art forms as the basis of my writing.

Like many quotes, the words in this book originated far deep within me and reflect my emotional state at a particular moment. The quotes are such that the reader does not need to be an artist or have any interest in art to make sense of what I have written.

This book is another in a series of publications that showcase my different interests—literary and visual arts—and allow me to share my inner thoughts with those who happen to come across my works.

To make the most of this book, it is advisable that you read one or two pages at a time, meditate on the words, and return to the book again and again.

Again, thank you for showing interest in my work as the writer and artist J. Bonegard.

1.

"For every artist, there are moments of breakthrough when what is depicted on the surface of a canvas is no more an ordinary image but an expression of inner truth and self-discovery."

J. Bonegard (2024)

2.

"I never understood the saying, 'happiness is a choice' until I met a man who lost it all once, only to find it in a painting."

J. Bonegard (2024)

3.

"I like to consider my abstract painting as the equivalent of a mathematical equation with one or more missing variables waiting to be solved by the observer."

J. Bonegard (2024)

4.

"When I paint, I lose my mother tongue and speak a language that is universal to all, one that requires the silence of the soul to give meaning to that which is physical and visible on a canvas."

J. Bonegard (2024)

5.

"An artist's masterpiece is what happens when painting meets with inspiration - not before, but during the act of painting."

J. Bonegard (2024)

6.

"Beyond the pictorial representation of my abstract paintings, I often imagine an invisible compilation of divination texts with enough power to bestow the onlooker with the gifts of happiness, peace, protection, and health."

J. Bonegard (2024)

7.

"What I paint means nothing until someone, somewhere, establishes the connection with what is revealed on a surface. To some, it is simply a painting, but others see it differently, something more intriguing and personal."

J. Bonegard (2024)

8.

"I consider myself and my paintings work in progress, where even though we are fully formed, we continue to evolve - me, in the perception of the world around me, and my paintings, in how they are perceived by the world that surrounds them."

J. Bonegard (2024)

9.

"In my work as a visual artist, I am often reminded of the plights of many, who for just and unjust reasons, are deprived of their freedom - physical, emotional, and spiritual."

J. Bonegard (2024)

10.

"To become the artist of my dream, I had to overcome the mystery of an illusion to reclaim my true destiny."

J. Bonegard (2024)

11.

"A painting commemorative
of a historic day in the life of
an artist is a special gift that
an artist should remember
to give to him or herself."

J. Bonegard (2024)

12.

"In creating a piece of abstract painting, my ambition is to create visibility for the unseen and give meaning to the incomprehensible."

J. Bonegard (2024)

13.

"When creating a painting, I know when I am being a coward and know when I am being brave, but on each occasion, I can never predict which one I would be."

J. Bonegard (2024)

14.

"You need not good eyes to appreciate what I paint, but you need a good heart to comprehend the thoughts behind the painting."

J. Bonegard (2024)

15.

"Nothing epitomizes the power of having a second chance as in the act of painting, where with every brushstroke that goes haywire, there is often another chance to restore order."

J. Bonegard (2024)

16.

"I paint with the future as my horizon and having a full glimpse of a moment in time when people who come across the painting would share sentiments similar to those surrounding its creation."

J. Bonegard (2024)

———————————————

17.

"When a newly completed abstract painting seems familiar, it is the closest I have come to experience déjà-vu in my studio art practice."

J. Bonegard (2024)

18.

"In my studio art practice, of all emotions, rarely have I been successful at creating an abstract painting that beautifully captures the emotion of joy."

J. Bonegard (2024)

19.

"To best appreciate my work, ignore the title of the painting and what it was made of, but stand still until you can feel its impact on your imagination, emotion, and thoughts."

J. Bonegard (2024)

20.

"The ephemeral nature of dreams ensures that an artist, despite his or her best effort, would never fully capture the true meaning of a dream."

J. Bonegard (2024)

____

21.

"As humans, the purest of imagination is only attainable when we forget who we are, ignore where we have been, and disregard where we are going."

J. Bonegard (2024)

22.

"In every breath is enough air to inspire the artist in me, enough fuel to maintain my zeal to create, and enough spark to power my curiosity for knowledge."

J. Bonegard (2024)

23.

"No one speaks the truth
like a child, and to paint like
a child is to speak the
absolute truth."

J. Bonegard (2024)

24.

"The marvel of a masterpiece lies in the fact that neither the artist nor the observer can predict what would become of a painting until much later in its existence."

J. Bonegard (2024)

25.

"As an artist, I dissect truth, not follow, question rhetoric, not follow, and examine motive, not follow."

J. Bonegard (2024)

26.

"Working a canvas is a reminder of a spiritual battle, akin to Jacob's wrestle with God, where the ultimate goal is to reveal my purpose and fulfill my destiny."

J. Bonegard (2024)

27.

"Many talk about sharing their testimonies, but I never thought of a better way to share mine than in the form of a painting to inspire others."

J. Bonegard (2024)

28.

"Of the many emotions that drive my creativity, anger is never one of them, for to surrender to anger is to be a victim twice over - first, as an individual, second, as a painting for others to see."

J. Bonegard (2024)

29.

"Contemplating whether to write a poem, I chose a language that needs no translation, a palette foreign to none, and a painting that says it all. This is my poem."

J. Bonegard (2024)

30.

"Being an artist means to be cognizant of how powerful art can be in communicating with people far removed from me and how a work of art is capable of eliciting the most complex of human emotions."

J. Bonegard (2024)

____

31.

"Every painting endeavor, no matter how small, is a deep dive into my emotions, hoping to capture the inexpressible in its physical form and give the ephemeral a lasting representation."

J. Bonegard (2024)

32.

"I started life as a dreamer
but stopped dreaming when
I caught the virus called
ambition, and not until I
discovered my paintbrush
that I began to dream
again."

J. Bonegard (2024)

33.

"To paint against hope is to keep painting when the odds are stacked against you, to keep your brushstrokes when others doubt, and to see a masterpiece when the majority is yet to see it."

J. Bonegard (2024)

34.

"There is no ordinary smile, for behind every facial expression lies buried a complexity of emotions (good and bad) and memories (recent and distant) that can never be deciphered by any stranger."

J. Bonegard (2024)

35.

"I sometimes recommend that viewers consider my painting part of an elixir where the accompanying quote and background music complete the magic."

J. Bonegard (2024)

36.

"As an artist, I have learned to let my dreams manifest in the moment by using my imagination to fill the void that exists between my aspiration and my reality."

J. Bonegard (2024)

37.

"In search of meaning, I nearly lost my freedom; in the search for freedom, I nearly lost my way, and in search of the way, I found art."

J. Bonegard (2024)

38.

"In my art studio practice, I often imagine a world where all we have at our disposal to communicate with fellow humans is the face, a world where no formal speech is required, and all humans have to rely on his facial expression."

J. Bonegard (2024)

39.

"In my studio art practice, there is often a time-lapse between creating a painting and gaining a full appreciation of what I had painted, how much more those encountering the work for the first time."

J. Bonegard (2024)

40.

"As humans, the purest of imagination is only attainable when we forget who we are, ignore where we have been, and disregard where we are going."

J. Bonegard (2024)

41.

"My art philosophy is such that painting geometric abstract enables my understanding of reality while painting other forms of abstract broadens my comprehension of immortality."

J. Bonegard (2024)

42.

"If all I have is a minute to say all that is on my mind, I will put all sixty seconds of it into an abstract painting; that way, I can say the most to everyone that matters."

J. Bonegard (2024)

43.

"I used to think being an artist meant I would have to grow up, but when I began to paint, I discovered that being an artist has more to do with unearthing my childhood sensibilities."

J. Bonegard (2024)

44.

"The eyes, as wonderful as they are for visual recognition, except in a rare minority, are totally useless when it comes to connecting to a human's soul, yet many unfamiliar with the way of the world seek answers in wrong places."

J. Bonegard (2024)

45.

"An abstract painting has the potential to fill the gulf where humans occasionally find themselves, serving as an interface between two diametric opposites - reality and fantasy, wellness and ill-health, joy and melancholy, pleasure and pain, justice and injustice, and many more."

J. Bonegard (2024)

46.

"Caught between somnolence and insomnia, I chose to paint; caught between dreaming and imagination, I chose to paint."

J. Bonegard (2024)

47.

"It's not how long you stare
at a painting that matters
but how long the emotion it
evokes takes to disappear
from your consciousness."

J. Bonegard (2024)

48.

"Assuming the myth that humans utilize less than ten percent of their brain for mentation is correct, it means I have over ninety percent of untapped cerebral assets for abstract painting."

J. Bonegard (2024)

———————————————————————

49.

"In my studio, whenever I
am caught between creating
an abstract painting or
abstraction, I can tell it's
time for a cup of tea."

J. Bonegard (2024)

50.

"Just like a precious painting hanging on a wall unrecognized, loneliness is like being invisible in a crowd."

J. Bonegard (2024)

51.

"I once thought painting was pure pleasure until I began painting from the depth of my pain, then I discovered that true pleasure is not always devoid of pain."

J. Bonegard (2024)

52.

"In my abstract paintings, I refuse to trust my eyes, nor trust my hands, but rely on intuition to do and undo what I see."

J. Bonegard (2024)

53.

"The miracle of this moment
lies in making it to the next,
for no one knows what the
future holds."

J. Bonegard (2024)

54.

"I paint abstract, never to challenge consciousness, but to evoke lurking emotions within the individual."

J. Bonegard (2024)

55.

"As an artist, I once painted to be seen, then painted to be heard; now, I paint in search of meaning."

J. Bonegard (2024)

56.

"I began my art journey by painting the obvious, then the less obvious, and now, I paint to discover hidden subtleties."

J. Bonegard (2024)

____

57.

"My paintings are no random acts but a ritual rooted in mixed emotions - joy, melancholy, optimism, nostalgia, and hope. Together, these elements make the perfect brew for my creative exploits."

J. Bonegard (2024)

58.

"As an artist, I have a greater appreciation of the closeness between what I think I know - perceived knowledge, and what I don't know that I do not know - unconscious ignorance."

J. Bonegard (2024)

59.

"My paintings are the result of conquests between the familiar and the unfamiliar, the intended and the accidental, and between the norm and the new normal."

J. Bonegard (2024)

60.

"Of all the verses of the Bible, there is none that touches my heart like that which had to with creation in Genesis 1:31. I quote - "Then God looked over all he had made, and he saw that it was very good! Genesis 1:31."

J. Bonegard (2024)

61.

"The artwork, titled Another Day in Paradise, the same name as a song by Phil Collins, was an abstraction depicting four humans lying in a relief of constrained space, evoking thoughts of homelessness and how many in our society, for varied reasons are one paycheck away from homelessness."

J. Bonegard (2024)

62.

"I never believed a picture is
worth a thousand words
until I painted the Garden of
Eden."

J. Bonegard (2024)

63.

"I once thought that lack of freedom meant being physically constrained but have since learned that many who are unbound in the physical realm are bound by other kinds of bondage."

J. Bonegard (2024)

64.

"An artist, once asked by a stranger to paint, left a blank canvas not knowing the stranger was an angel sent to anoint his/her hands."

J. Bonegard (2024)

____

65.

"As an artist, I find inspiration in all places, seek truth from all ages, and perceive answers in all faces."

J. Bonegard (2024)

66.

"I would like to say I know what I am doing when I paint, but I have since recognized a higher Force is holding my hand, directing my brushstrokes, and turning an ordinary painting into the work of a genius."

J. Bonegard (2024)

67.

"The book of the story of our lives is never complete without us leaving unfilled pages for those coming behind to complete."

J. Bonegard (2024)

68.

"My art, like the ordinary babble of a child that is loaded with meaning and readily deciphered by the mother, is purely for those who dare to listen."

J. Bonegard (2024)

69.

"Creativity is an exploit of
the soul - unsure you have
what it takes, and uncertain
where it takes you."

J. Bonegard (2024)

70.

"The law of human nature states that the evil that one human does to another is inversely proportional to the distance between them, with one singular exception - the presence of unconditional love."

J. Bonegard (2024)

71.

"When I paint, my prayer is that my art stirs the hearts of humans to turn their mind to those things which unite us all."

J. Bonegard (2024)

72.

"Survival is simply not the will to survive, but the determination to rise above the encumbrance of human nature."

J. Bonegard (2024)

73.

"In creating a work of art,
my ultimate goal is to
ensure that when the work
is completed, it will be
almost impossible to create
another that looks exactly
like it."

J. Bonegard (2024)

74.

"Hope is the sound you listen to when all that is happening around you makes no sense, but you do not want to lose faith in humanity."

J. Bonegard (2024)

75.

"As an artist, the joy of what
I do lies in the fact that I
start painting not knowing
where I am going but
confident that I would
recognize the destination
the moment it shows on the
horizon."

J. Bonegard (2024)

76.

"My work as an artist is incomplete until the thoughts that keep me awake at night become an inspiration for the artwork that I paint during the day."

J. Bonegard (2024)

77.

"How I survived for five decades without ever handling a paintbrush or creating a painting remains a subject of mystery."

J. Bonegard (2024)

78.

"If you ever find yourself alone on a desert island, remember your mind is a boundless territory, and imagination is how you get to your utopia."

J. Bonegard (2024)

79.

"The chemistry of the equilibrium of love is never static but subject to the effects of catalysts and inhibitors that define our nature as humans."

J. Bonegard (2024)

80.

"Thank God for Mondays,
for without its blues,
Tuesdays will be ordinary,
and Fridays will mean little
in our lives."

J. Bonegard (2024)

81.

"My greatest thoughts begin as thoughts about nothing - not things, not life or death, not even art but soon gravitate to thoughts of imagination, both great and small."

J. Bonegard (2024)

82.

"Art taught me that to quench my thirst, it is better to travel miles to get to the wellspring of imagination than to drink from the abundance of nostalgia."

J. Bonegard (2024)

83.

"To be filled with the joy of life is to be happy despite all without reason."

J. Bonegard (2024)

84.

"The bird in me sings: I had devoted my life to creating second chances for many; art became my golden opportunity of a second chance."

J. Bonegard (2024)

85.

"Look around to see if you can find that material object of sentimental value, more like a charm that speaks to your emotional self. If you don't, you are not alone, for many earthly treasures are locked up and hardly seen by those they are meant to serve."

J. Bonegard (2024)

86.

"I would rather lose my feathers than lose my mind, for outward elegance is no replacement for resplendence of the spirit."

J. Bonegard (2024)

87.

"The artist in me dictates that I pull the largest caravan ever where love is the only visible color."

J. Bonegard (2024)

88.

"I have listened to many songs and watched several concerts, but when art became my lullaby, I knew I had found heaven."

J. Bonegard (2023)

89.

"Choosing to see art simply in one dimension is like choosing to remain forever in a cradle."

J. Bonegard (2023)

90.

"To remain set in our old ways and resist change without reasoning is to forget our reason for being."

J. Bonegard (2023)

91.

"On the last days, when the gates of heaven finally open, after babies are let in, next will be artists, then the saints, and then others."

J. Bonegard (2023)

92.

"I never fully understood the true meaning of beauty until I stumbled across abstract art."

J. Bonegard (2023)

93.

"I was once taught that to dream, I needed to sleep, but the artist in me taught me to dream while I am still awake."

J. Bonegard (2023)

94.

"The heart of man,
whenever it overflows,
paints a picture of what lies
deep within the individual."

J. Bonegard (2023)

95.

"At certain times, human dignity is the universal language through which faith in humanity is expressed."

J. Bonegard (2023)

96.

Passion

"About me – a sense of completeness.
About others – the opportunity to serve.
About today – a reason to carry on.
About tomorrow – a future to aspire to.
About money – enough to make a living.
About ambition – need no position.
About ego – not about me.
About the world – all about humanity.
About philosophy – a life of meaning.
About spirituality – a reason for being."

J. Bonegard (2023)

97.

"Destiny is a mystery, often mired in a fierce conquest as fate and faith battle for the truth."

J. Bonegard (2023)

98.

"Art is the only way I know
to stay young - at heart, in
spirit, and truth."

J. Bonegard (2023)

____

99.

"December 12 will never be the same again; despite betrayal and injustice, hope surely must endure."

J. Bonegard (2023)

100.

"When two sincere spirits
act in unison to do good,
peace reigns."

J. Bonegard (2023)

ARTIST

- J. Bonegard - surgeon, turned artist.

- outré-chirurgie (beyond-surgery)

- exploring vagaries of art perception and dreams, (and quotes)

  "risk something - discover my art"

  – J. Bonegard (2022)

To learn more about the artist J. Bonegard, visit www.jbonegard.com

www.ingramcontent.com/pod-product-compliance
Lightning Source LLC
Chambersburg PA
CBHW071224260726

48653CB00042B/2035